Reflections

Monica Czerniak

BookLeaf Publishing

Presentation by *BookLeaf Publishing*

Web: www.bookleafpub.com

E-mail: info@bookleafpub.com

ISBN: 9789357211840

First edition 2023

DEDICATION

I dedicate this book to my parents who
encourage me to write and to be true to myself.

Blank Cards

In his wallet, he carries business cards,
coal black, with no text, no nothing,
on either side.
His fingers, long as grasshopper legs,
store them in his left breast pocket,
the place where he pulls out his neatly
stacked 5-dollar bills to pay me for a coffee.

He asks me what I can offer him
in black.
I laugh.
This is a café after all, I say.

He hands his business cards
to all he chooses to talk to.
Randomly.
Deliberately.
From behind my counter I watch him carefully,
with steam rising from the espresso machine.

He walks with a gait that inspires
roses to wilt and cats to purr.
He pulls out the cards from his breast pocket
with mischievous fingers wanting to play.

I take my break, sit and stare blankly,
stirring my spoon into the bleak, black brew.
I feel his presence approaching.
I hear the shaking of his breast pocket for a card.
My turn is now.
What question will he ask me?

His black wild eyes lock with mine like
two magic eight balls.
He hands me a card.
Yes or no? he asks.
I say yes.

We pause.

He smiles as I take his card and slide it
between my two front teeth.
Namelessfacelessblackandblank.

Your Love

3

More
Love
Curved
Lips
Luring
Eyes
The smell of skin
Warm skin
Legs
Tangled
Under
Blankets
Where all has become light again
Raising the tiny hairs behind the neck
Like blades of grass in the spring.

Insomniatic Thoughts

1.
You see me
I see you too.
I never understood what that meant,
until I met you.

2.
In this pale light
I live and I die
what feels like a few thousand lives.

3.
I love the night
it covers me with its cool blanket
and reminds me to keep going with its stars.

Applause

5

How strange it was
to hear fluttering wings
ricocheting off my bedroom walls.
It was as if the birds applaud me
like an audience clapping for an encore.

As I rose from my bed that morning
I almost felt as if I had accomplished something in my sleep.
I bowed my head
looked at my toes
and put on some socks.
Godspeed.

Snowflakes

Over a very strong black coffee
served with a little extra something
we laughed and ate all the cookies.

All sorts of life had happened
the sun forgot to rise
as we danced underground Manhattan
the night was ours.

Snowflakes fell unexpectedly
a bartender bit my hand told me I was pretty
we pondered life and its meaning
what being alive meant to us really
just a thought.

You then lost your favorite bracelet
wondered if it fell off
or was stolen while in that basement
we paused.

The sun then winked between the buildings
a flurried light sparkled as those snowflakes
we threw a penny in that fountain
smiled, parted, and said nothing.

**Snowflakes can be listened to on my debut album
"littleuniverses" .

After the Party

7

Morning has broken
the sun coats the earth
like powdered sugar on a jelly donut.
I close the door behind me
and confuse the smell of old beer for a human.

Escape Plan: Conversation

In that one moment
your voice triggered such repulsion in me
I couldn't stand the sight of you any longer
I needed to leave.
While your lips motioned words
I saw the door's reflection in your irises
there was a way out.
I started to list every step of my escape plan in my mind:

First I would take my bicycle and pedal until I was out of breath,
then drop it and hop in a taxi whose last client left the door open,
then catch a chartered bus out of the city leaving express,
then take a fast train off the island
and start to picture life without you as far away as I can.

After thinking about how romantic the idea
of sitting peacefully on a train in absence of you was,
I imagined registering my name for the next rocket ship to Mars
It just felt right.
I was feeling confident with this plan of action,
I must have smirked.
At that moment you asked me if I was OK,
I coughed and said I was fine.

Roadtrip

There is calmness in the air outside
the morning sun nudges the sky and reminds us of the time
we buzz like the creatures within the dewy lawn.
You take my bag and head to the car
our destination 300 miles south from our cool north.
I look you in the eyes
the birds answer
the engine purrs
I smile with my hand on your thigh.

We roll until the roads become broad and then thin again
until cities transform to towns and houses become barns
we roll until fields meet mountains
while the radio plays us a score.
Your palms have taken on the mold of the wheel
your shoulder the mold of my head.
Creamy cotton clouds stream along the ever-changing sky
as we journey into mountains where wolves howl and deer graze
signs alert us for moose.

I open the window to feel speed with my hands
the thick wet country air streams between my fingers
firework colored leaves signal
the height of the mountains and change in climate
clouds now appear to us as mountains in the distance
my ears pop and you pull over
you tell me that we are almost there
your fingers clasp onto mine
the sun has reached its zenith
we pour coffee from the thermos.

Summer Bonfire

Around the fire
we sat
in a circle
catching sparks
on our legs
watching flames dance
against the night sky
feeling alive and
well.

Insurance

I went for a walk at 8pm
once darkness had set
the sound of screeching tires
traveled through the air
I realized that I was but seconds away
from all that could have never been my life.
My hands upon the hood of the car
I looked up at the windshield,
the driver dumbfounded told me
that it was a good thing
they didn't have to use their insurance on this incident.
I then wondered what the value of my life was.

Curvy Lines

I outlined a path
when its lines began to fade
I traced back my steps
and questioned if lines needed to be straight.
That night my hands touched my chest
like they belonged to someone else,
such tenderness I had only felt
when I replied that I would never tell what you revealed.
I understood then
that our lines could never lead
down a path that was straight.
That was then
now we have drafted lines
leading to where we would never meet again
knowing that lines don't need to be straight.

Aftershock

13

Whatever happened
Is now in embers
Warm
Condensed
Fragments of past
In pieces
From one
to many
to few
burning.

Belief and Pragmatism

Many times
the me, myself and I
whisper inwardly that I can do "it"
and watch the past, present and future
blinking, wincing and winking.
Raising my chin
I search for the untouchable,
grasp the attainable
then get blackened by the soot of rationality.
The romantic in me wants to believe.
There is so much beauty in belief.
After practicing self-reliance as a form of spirituality
I fold in all three and hold them tightly to my heart
buttering bread, drinking wine
and with an open palm
sagaciously repeating
believing in me myself and I.

In Memory of Us

I still appreciate Britten, Pho Soup,
And laugh thinking about the bags of jelly beans
we used to eat while studying.
How we fumbled around
with our intellectual dreams
experiencing a coming of age
I doubt you would ever admit that.

I like to think about the dance you used to do for me
where you would spin around like flying saucer
being funny and smart
I think you have probably kept those qualities.

Then
there
are
two
years
of
my
life
that
I
don't
remember
much of.

Now my hair is long
I have found a new home in my skin
I don't think we will ever talk again
I think that it is better that way
I lit a candle today,
And let it speak in memory of us and all that we were.

Toxicity

I.
The sound of your voice
Corrupts me
Like a magnet to a hard drive
I hear it
And go blank
II.
You covered me with your shadow
as a blanket
When I let in the light
I finally saw that your true color was blank
III.
You left your trace
like an old scripture
and blackened
the lining
in the cave of my heart

Folklore

17

Pain is not my defender
Love is not my savior
You told me you wanted me
Except you wanted to skip chapters

I placed love on the top shelf
In a jar far to touch
I hid it there safely
As relationships proved to cause floods

I'm not searching for your ruins
But I know how to dig
Found a few bones in your closet
My hope proved to be a dangerous thing

Took out my guitar
When in came a bird
Who flew to the jar (seemed to know where my love was)
It pecked as I plucked
Soon love won me over

Brooding

I spun a yellow pencil
with your tooth marks
on my table
to encourage
a dream
without a direction.
As I watched the pencil's pink tip eraser circle and spin
I summoned up syllables
Of our last conversation.
Much to my dismay
The pencil spun
into the wastebasket.
That's when I knew
There was truly nothing left
To hold on to.

E-Archetype

Expressing
Silence
Nonchalance
Coping.

Failing fast forward
At what expense;
Life can be so expensive.

Moving inward
Meandering
Being expansive.

Honestly
Exhaustingly
Recharging.

www.ingramcontent.com/pod-product-compliance
Lightning Source LLC
LaVergne TN
LVHW050310200726
843509LV00015B/3267